PRIMARY PRODIGIES

Chapter One

By: Robert and Samantha Young

Illustrations: Robert Young with art licensed at FreePik.com

All rights reserved. No part of this publication may be reproduced, stored in a retrieval system, or transmitted by any means without the express permission of Preschool Prodigies and Young Music, LLC.
Published by: Young Music, LLC
ISBN: 978-0999210185
Copyright © 2017
Preschool Prodigies and Young Music, LLC
2358 Dutch Neck Road
Smyrna, DE 19977

Welcome to Primary Prodigies!

Hello there and welcome to Primary Prodigies Chapter 1.

Primary Prodigies is a fun and colorful approach to music. If you've ever been curious about singing, playing an instrument, or about performing in a show, you'll need to know the concepts in this book.

The language of music is very big and learning all the sounds can be hard. In this book, you'll see how with just 8 notes, 3 chords, and 4 different rhythms, we can make all kinds of music.

Lots of people think learning music is dificult, but it's not! It's fun and natural and something that lives inside all of us!

Reading sheet music... that can be hard, and that's where a lot of people stop playing their instrument.

Don't worry... that's not going to happen here. Most of the sheet music in this book is color-coded, so if you're using the bells, a piano with stickers, or even a guitar with stickers, you'll always know what notes you're reading on the page.

We also make reading the rhythms in this book very easy, and with the help of the videos inside the Prodigies Playground, you'll be able to follow along easily.

If you've ever sat at the piano and wanted to know how the notes work together, soon you will know! And if you've ever wanted to write some music of your own, we'll be doing a bit of that, too!

Here in Chapter 1, we'll meet the different musical notes, learn a little bit about how the notes work together, about how to read rhythms, and we'll also learn about the Solfege Hand-Signs.

If you've completed Preschool Prodigies, this Chapter will be a bit of a review, as well as the start of a more advanced music education. Primary Prodigies features a lot more vocabulary, more detailed explanations of the concepts, and the videos are much longer!

If you've not completed Preschool Prodigies, definitely check out the next page for a good outline of how to use the program.

If you're brand new to the Playground, you might want to drop by Chapter 8 of Preschool Prodigies to warm up a little bit.

You may also use Preschool Chapter 7 to review chords and PsP Melodies to review the Solfege Hand-Signs. In fact, almost all of the Preschool Prodigies videos will work to reinforce and expand the concepts in Primary Prodigies, so don't be shy about visiting those videos as well if you want some more introductory material.

Using Primary Prodigies

This workbook is a companion to the videos found at PreschoolProdigies.com/Play. Using the videos and this book together, you will be making music in no-time!

To make the most out of Primary Prodigies, follow the steps below for each section of the series:

1. Watch the Video(s)
Start by watching the videos that go with each section. For Primary Prodigies, start with the "lesson" video to learn a bit about what's coming up. Then replay the "song" video as often as it takes to really master playing along.

2. Play the Sheet Music
After you've played the video once or twice, try playing the sheet music found in this book. You might find it easier to read the sheet music, or maybe you'll find it easier to play with the help of the video. Either way, you'll want to get comfortable playing it both ways. The video will help you keep a steady beat and you'll need to learn to read from the sheet music for future music making!

3. Complete the Activities
After playing through the sheet music, complete the pencil-and-paper activities that follow. Keep your instrument nearby and grab some crayons or colored pencils to match the colors of the notes.

4. Practice Repetition Until Mastery
Continue to practice with the video and the sheet music until you can sing and play the song with confidence and accuracy. You might think that playing the same song over and over is boring, but if you ever want to perform a piece of music in front of an audience, you'll definitely want to practice that piece A LOT.

The same way athletes practice everyday to become the best, repetition with your instrument builds musical muscles in your body and sparks all kinds of awesome brain activity.

Every musician has a list of songs they know and love to play and we call that list a repertoire. Your repertoire will be full of your favorite songs, and you'll want to practice them over and over so you're ready to play them for friends and family.

The songs and concepts in this book are just the beginning of this series. As we get into later Chapters of Primary Prodigies, we'll be building a repertoire of classical music, popular songs, and Prodigies originals so that you'll be ready for all kinds of musical events! Make sure to really master the concepts in this book, and you'll be on your way to all kinds of musical greatness!

Happy Musicing!

- Mr. Rob

1.1 – Hello Bells Introduction

Play along with video 1.1 using this sheet music! Alternate between playing your bells, singing the notes, singing the numbers and singing the lyrics. Can you pronounce the different ways to say "Hello" around the world?

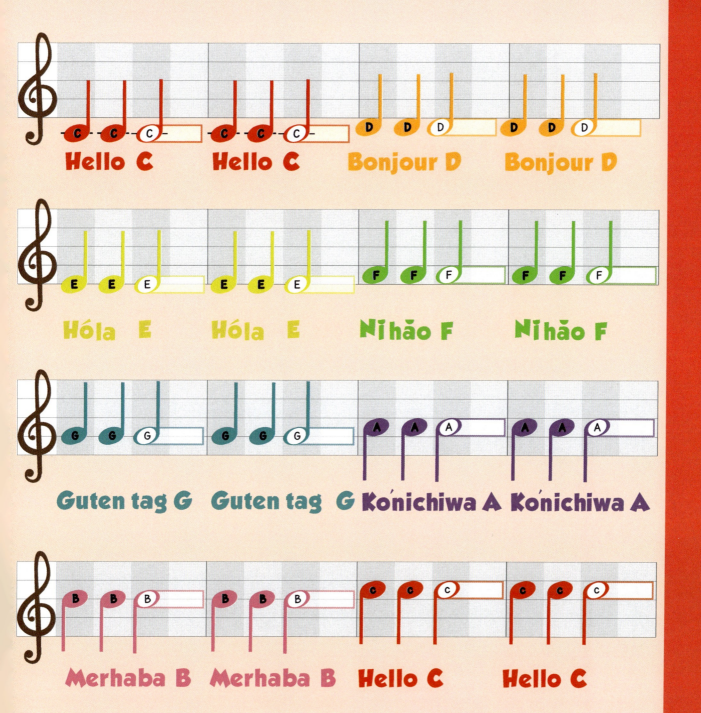

Review and Introductory Activities

The activities that follow will familiarize you with the 8 musical notes we met in the 1.1 videos. They will also review some of the activities and concepts from both Preschool Prodigies & PsP Melodies, so if you have trouble with this section, definitely review Chapter 1, 4 and 8 from Preschool Prodigies and some of PsP Melodies!

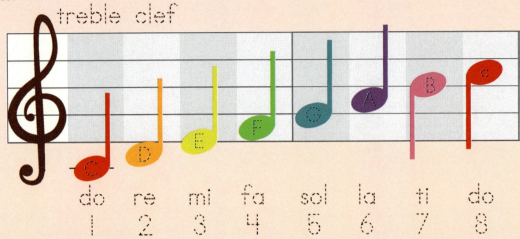

Which Note : Part I

In 1.1, we played 8 musical notes on the Treble Clef. For now, they are color coded and labeled to make it as easy as possible, but as you get further into the workbook, the activities will become more difficult.

For now, you can use the picture above to help you answer the following questions!

A: Fill in the letter names on the lines above.

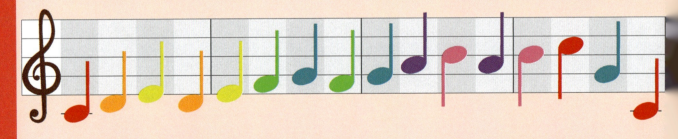

B: Fill in the Solfege syllables names on the lines above.

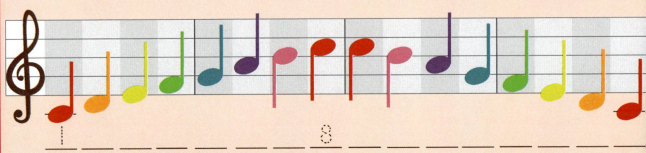

C: Fill in the Scale Degrees (numbers) on the lines above.

Which Note : Part II ✏️

Uh oh! The notes have lost their color. Can you circle the correct color that goes with each note? We practiced some activities like this in PsP Melodies and Preschool Prodigies, but if you're unsure, move on for now and give it a try at the end of the chapter.

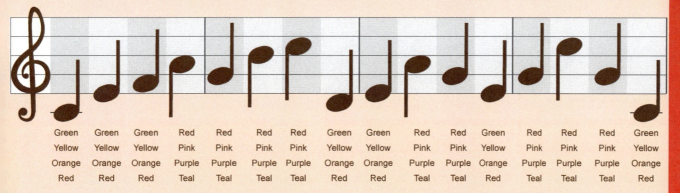

Green	Green	Green	Red	Red	Red	Red	Green	Green	Red	Red	Green	Red	Red	Red	Green
Yellow	Yellow	Yellow	Pink	Pink	Pink	Pink	Yellow	Yellow	Pink	Pink	Yellow	Pink	Pink	Pink	Yellow
Orange	Orange	Orange	Purple	Purple	Purple	Purple	Orange	Orange	Purple	Purple	Orange	Purple	Purple	Purple	Orange
Red	Red	Red	Teal	Teal	Teal	Teal	Red	Red	Teal	Teal	Red	Teal	Teal	Teal	Red

The Staff as our Musical Map ✏️

Music is written on a STAFF, and when we don't have color-coded music, the STAFF becomes our musical map! The higher a note is on the staff, the higher the note is going to sound!

The STAFF is made up of 5 LINES and 4 SPACES. Say it out loud... "5 Lines and 4 Spaces."

Do you see how the staff is made of 5 lines and 4 spaces? Don't forget that the higher sounding notes are higher on the staff!

1. Using a pencil, mark each line or space with an X. This will help you start to become familiar with our musical map, the STAFF.

Line 3   Line 1   Space 1   Space 4   Line 2   Line 5   Space 2   Space 3

2. Most music NOTES look like little ovals. Practice writing some simple musical notes (ovals) on the following lines and spaces.

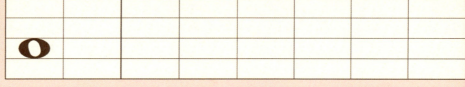

Space 2   Line 1   Space 1   Space 4   Line 2   Line 5   Space 2   Space 3

3. Notes that are higher on the staff also sound higher! In this activity, look at the second NOTE in each MEASURE and circle whether it's HIGHER or LOWER.

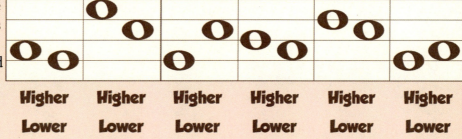

Higher   Higher   Higher   Higher   Higher   Higher
Lower   Lower   Lower   Lower   Lower   Lower

Get to Know the Staff!

This is the staff. This is where all of our musical notes live!

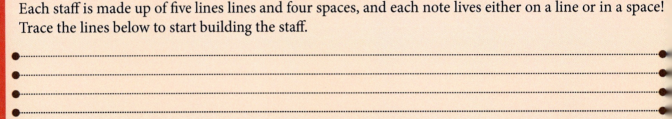

Lines and Space ✏️

Each staff is made up of five lines lines and four spaces, and each note lives either on a line or in a space! Trace the lines below to start building the staff.

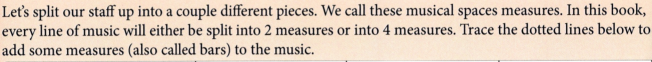

Adding Measures ✏️

Let's split our staff up into a couple different pieces. We call these musical spaces measures. In this book, every line of music will either be split into 2 measures or into 4 measures. Trace the dotted lines below to add some measures (also called bars) to the music.

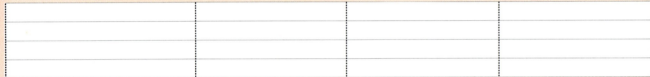

The Treble Clef ✏️

The TREBLE CLEF is a very famous music symbol. Practice tracing it below! Also, notice how the Treble Clef curls over the note G. That will help us figure out what notes we have even without color.

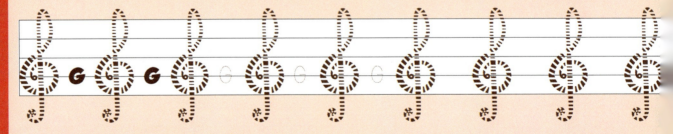

4 Beats Per Measure ✏️

Most of the measures in this book will have 4 beats each. The music in this book uses gray boxes to help make the beats easier to see. Write the numbers 1 through 4 in each box, just like the first measure.

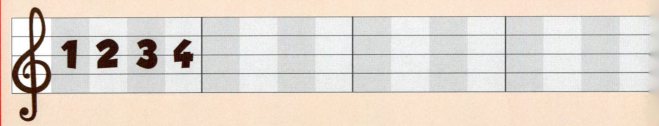

Musical Note Fill in the Blanks ✏️

Can you correctly identify each of the notes below? Complete the story below by writing the note names on the lines below. Use the colors to guide you, or else don't forget that the treble clef curls over the note G.

1.2 - Hot Cross Buns Review

Play, sing and hand-sign along with each of the songs from the 1.2 video: "Hot Cross Buns", "Merrily We Roll Along" and "Sally the Camel". You'll see some faster notes in measure 3 called eighth notes. Play along with the video to learn how these eighth notes feel.

HOT CROSS BUNS

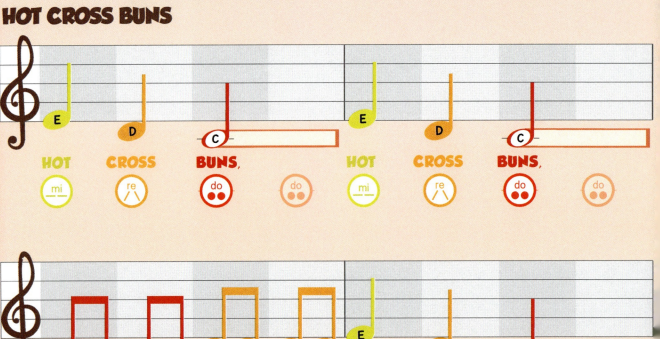
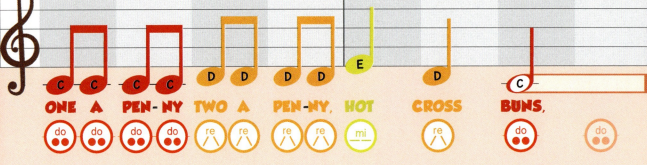
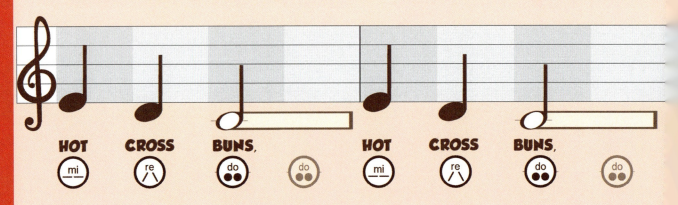

1.2 – Merrily We Roll Along Review

1.2 – Sally the Camel Review

The rhythm in the beginning of this song can be a little tricky, but if you practice it with the video, you'll hear how it goes. It starts with two fast eighth notes, then takes a short eighth note rest, before playing more of the same note. It's almost like playing seven notes in a row, but skipping over the 3rd.

SALLY THE CAMEL

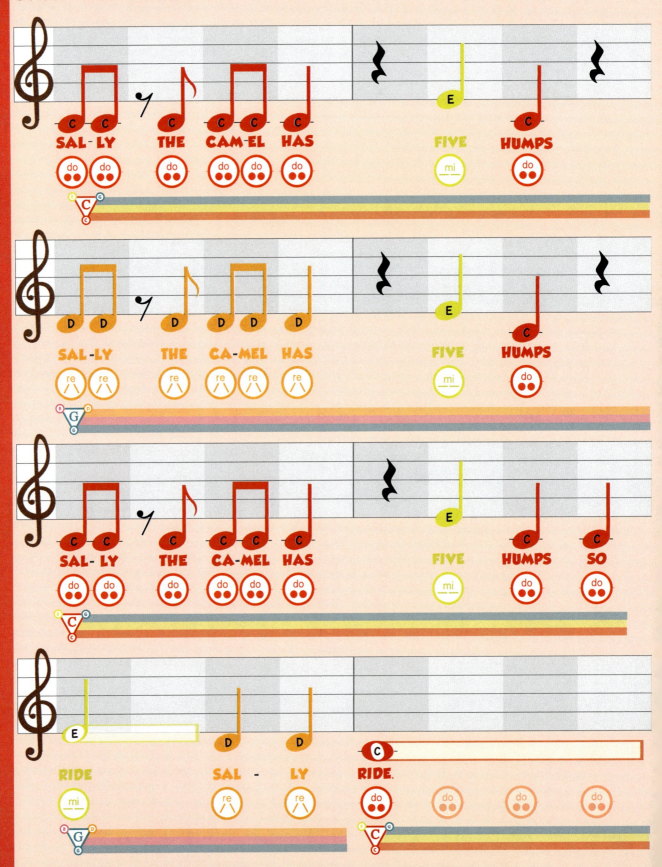

Music Word Search

Can you find all of the hidden words listed below? You should be able to find all 12 words, just moving backwards, forwards, up and down.

```
G F O F W D L X P K P L M Q C P H V X S
S F E C U I H V C L E F O Y K M M Q U I
W A L C B N V U A P L I N E S J K C U F
R T A J S Z B V X I L V N Q A V E W P U
T S C Z R Z B T A X Z W L H Z A E N S R
R S S G K D C R J J L H J G F Y K K G K
E E A H G M V S T S E R W S B J R L E U
R C Z U T Y H M H V G S W A Y G Z S E O
U A Z G Q Q R G L B E P Y I E C F U Y B
S P B W M M S Y R G F R D Q L M U D P A
A S X T V J U E S W L C J F R Z G V E R
E D N R B O W U Y O M G I Q E L I Z Y
M K J E S T H E D W S O N G S Q S W X P
B U Z B U N R K W Z Q Z H P E E U C D C
E P P L F S D B A C P P K U T W G V X D
G N H E A V R B V J B W X R O W A Y J F
L G L Y Z R U Y C T Q O F R N I K Z A I
Q G L V H X N Z M Z K M A V S J S R E W
M S K P X D Q N F P W I O X S O P F R P
T R I H J F N X G D O D B Q X N G N O Z
```

TREBLE	CLEF	STAFF
BAR	MEASURE	LINES
SPACES	NOTES	RESTS
SOLFEGE	SCALE	SONGS

Draw Each Note

Using the note names listed below, draw each note in the correct location on the staff. If you have a hard time, turn back to the previous page for hints!

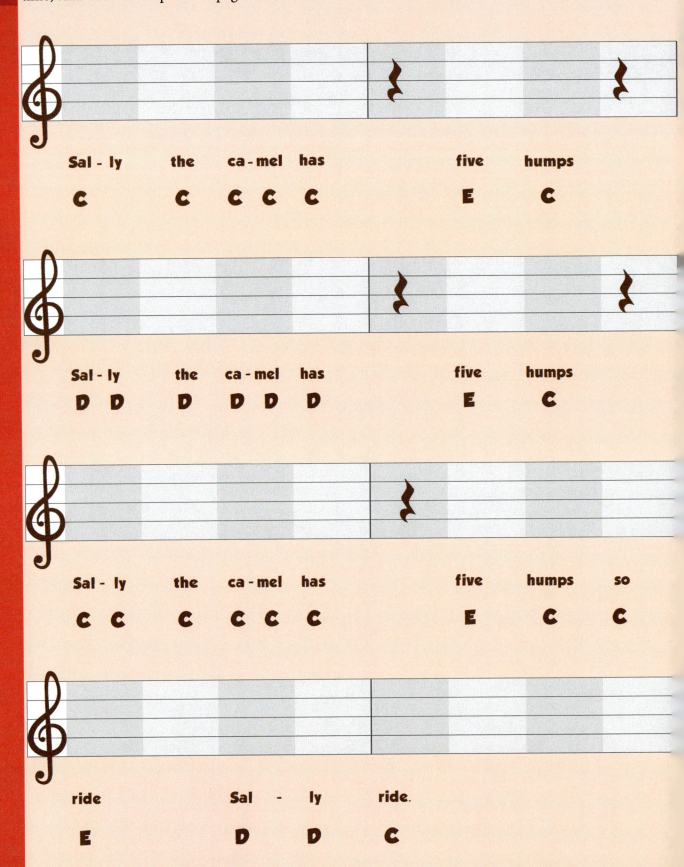

Hot cross buns, Hot cross buns,
E D C E D C

One a pen-ny two a pen-ny, hot cross buns,
C C C C D D D D E D C

Mer - ri - ly we roll a long
E D C D E E E

on the deep blue sea.
D D E D C

16 Identify Each Note

After looking at each note, write each note name below each note. Try not to look at any resources or song sheets to complete this activity.

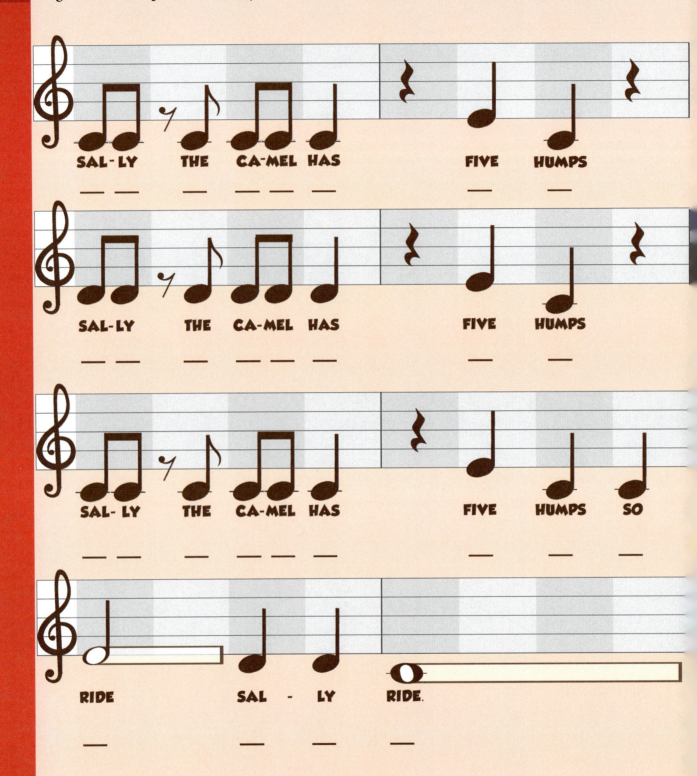

1.3 Sweet Beets with Watermelon, Melon, Beet & Cherry

The fruit and vegetable rhythms from Sweet Beets are below! Can you read and play them? If you have trouble, play along with the video. Use a metronome to help you stay in time.

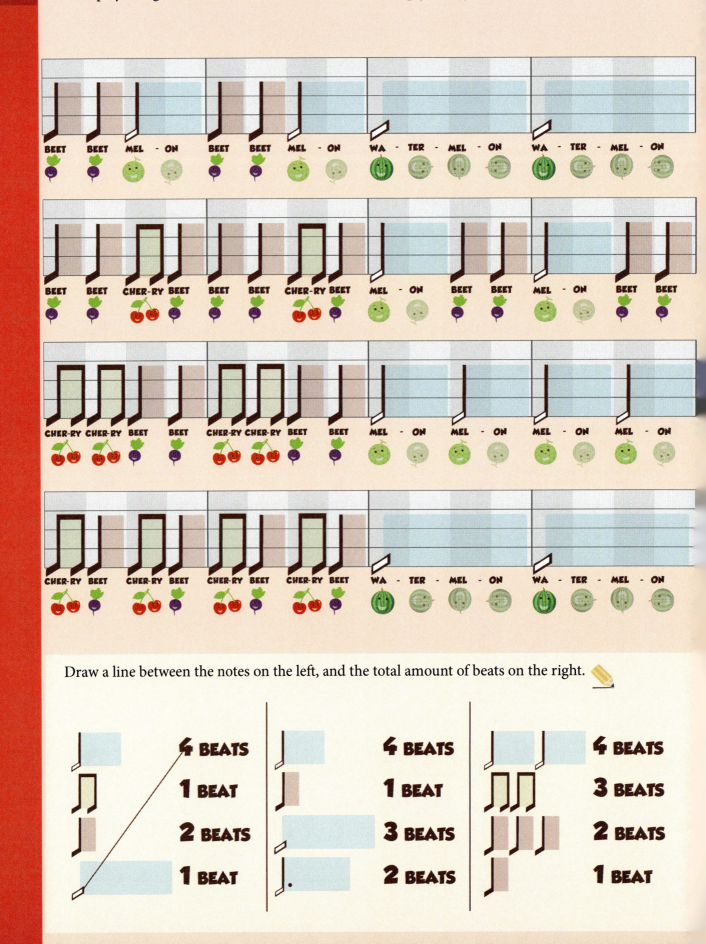

Draw a line between the notes on the left, and the total amount of beats on the right.

Nice job with the fruit and vegetable rhythms! This page has the same pattern of rhythms, but this time, we'll sing some different lyrics.
First we sing the name of the note lengths, like quarter half and whole. Then we move on to counting out loud with the numbers of the beat! The number system at the end is the most advanced and professional way of talking about rhythms, so make sure you get to the end of the page.

Challenge: How many beats (gray boxes) does each note take up?

20 Draw the Missing Note

Some of the following measures are missing a note! Can you correctly identify the missing notes and add them to their incomplete measures? The colored boxes will give you hints!

Rhythm Vocabulary Matching: Part I

Can you draw a line between each type of note and how many beats it represents?

EIGHTH NOTE				FOUR BEATS

QUARTER NOTE			ONE BEAT

HALF NOTE				ONE-HALF BEATS

WHOLE NOTE				TWO BEATS

Beat Math ✏️

Review the challenge on page 19 and study how much each beat is worth. Then, add each beat below according to its musical space value. Bonus: Can you add FIVE beats together?

♩ + ♩ =   𝅗𝅥 + 𝅗𝅥 =   ♩ + ♩ + ♩ =

♩ + 𝅗𝅥 =   𝅗𝅥 + ♩ =   ♩ + ♩ + ♩ =

♩ + ♩ =   ♩ + ♩ =   ♩ + ♩ + ♩ =

♩ + ♩ =   ♩ + ♩ =   ♩ + 𝅗𝅥 + ♩ =

𝅗𝅥 + ♩ =   ♩ + ♩ =   𝅗𝅥 + ♩ + ♩ =

♩ + ♩ =   ♩ + 𝅗𝅥 =   ♩ + 𝅗𝅥 + ♩ =

♩ + ♩ =   ♩ + ♩ =   ♩ + ♩ + ♩ =

𝅗𝅥 + ♩ =   𝅗𝅥 + 𝅗𝅥 =   𝅗𝅥 + ♩ + 𝅗𝅥 =

♩ + ♩ + 𝅗𝅥 + ♩ + ♩ =

𝅗𝅥 + 𝅗𝅥 + ♩ + 𝅗𝅥 + ♩ =

22 Eliminate the Extra Note ✏️

Each of the measures below has an extra note added by mistake! Find the extra note and draw an X through it.

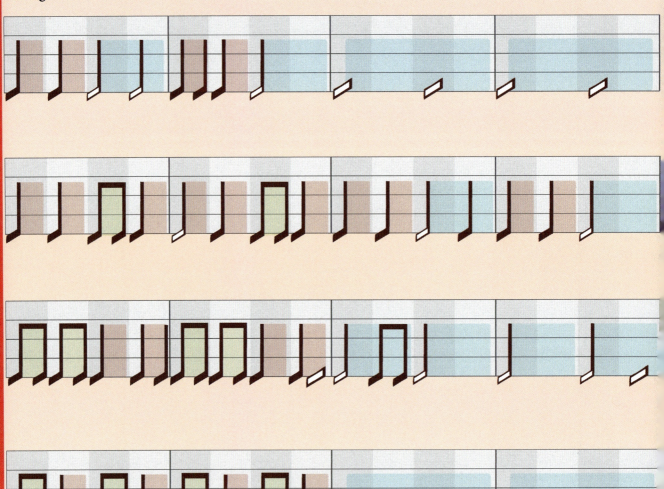

Rhythm Vocabulary Matching: Part II ✏️

Can you draw a line between each rhythm word and it's definition?

COUNTING OUT LOUD   MUSICAL SPACE

MEASURE   MACHINE THAT KEEPS THE BEAT

TEMPO   BEATS PER MINUTE

METRONOME   SAYING THE RHYTHMS YOU PLAY

BPM   SPEED OF THE MUSIC

Beat Math: Level 2 ✏️

Now that you've practiced adding beats together, try these harder variations of four and five beats. As a bonus question, can you add TEN beats together?

1.4 – Musical Steps

After you watch the 1.4 video, try playing along with the sheet music! Practice hand-signs & chords using the symbols below each note. For an extra challenge, the second half of the song has no color! Don't worry, the second verse is the same, but challenge yourself to see if you can read the music with no color.

26 Up, Down and Same Multiple Choice

In each of the rectangles below, there is an example of one of the following: a step up, a step down or a same step. Choose A, B or C to correctly identify the image in each rectangle.

28 Musical Steps Review ✏️

Draw each Solfege hand-sign above the correct note and number. If you can't remember the hand signs, look back at your sheet music for Five Little Pumpkins!

TIP: If you're having trouble with the step activities, think of the notes on actual stairs as shown here. If the notes are next to each other, they are only one step apart!

In the next lesson, we'll explore musical skips, which is when you jump from one note and then OVER another note. Come back to this page if you need a reminder about which notes are a step away.

The Stepping Song ✏️

Use the staffs below to write your own song. Challenge yourself to use only step ups, step downs or notes that stay the same. After you draw the notes, be sure to label your song with arrows and play your tune on the bells! For a bonus, add some lyrics to your stepping song.

Let's Take a Closer Look at Your Song! ✏️

1. How many step ups do you count in your song? _____

2. How many step downs do you count in your song? _____

3. How many same steps do you count in your song? _____

4. How could you add variety or change your song? _____
   _____
   _____

30   5 Little Pumpkins, Stepping Up and Down

Now that you've practiced with musical steps quite a bit, let's try to identify the steps and the "same" movement in Five Little Pumpkins. Draw an arrow up, down or straight to show the motion of the song.

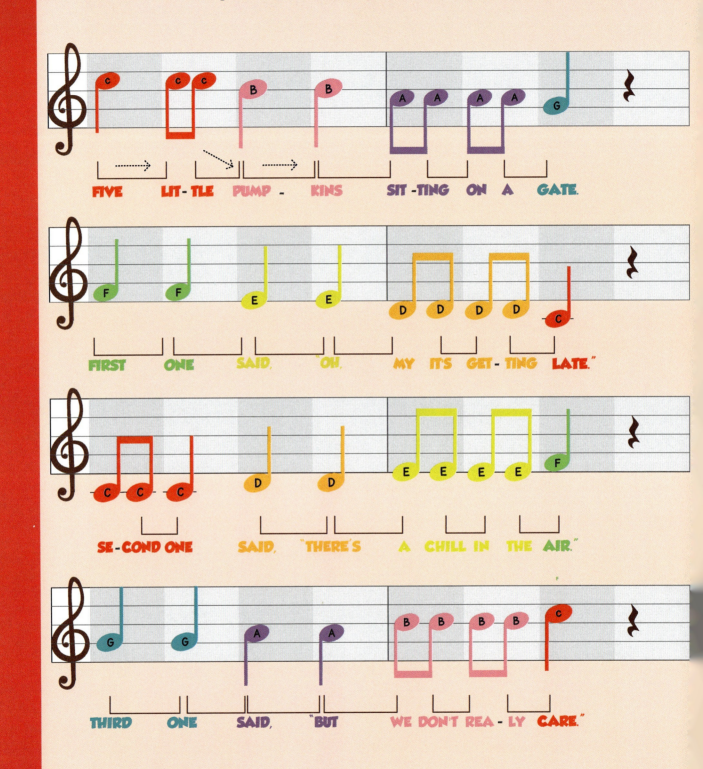

1.5 - Musical Skips

After you watch the 1.5 video, try playing along with the sheet music! You can sing about the letters, the colors, the numbers, or even practice with the Solfege Hand Signs! Then when you get to the next page, you'll definitely need your instrument!

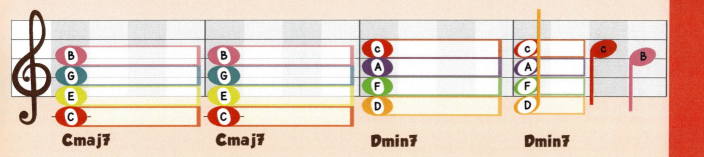
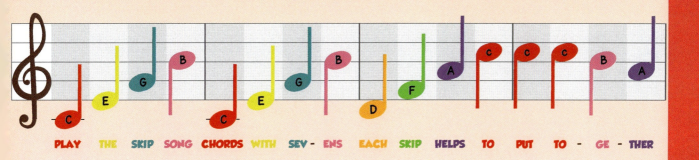
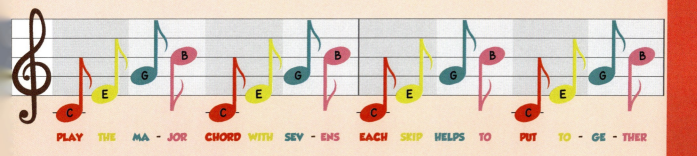
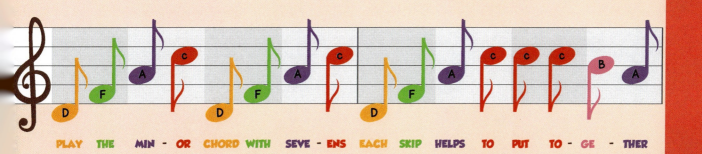

34 Musical Skips Multiple Choice

In each of the rectangles below, there is an example of one of the following: a skip up, a skip down or no skip. Choose A, B or C to correctly identify the image in each rectangle.

Draw the Note: Skip Up or Down

Let's draw some notes that skip! Look at the note in each measure. Then, draw either a note that skips up, or a note that skips down. Follow the direction above each line to find if we're skipping up or down.

Scale Degrees: Skip Up or Down

Let's try some more skips using our scale degrees (the numbers of the notes). If we start at 1 and skip up, we go over the next number (2) and land on 3. Make sure to read the heading of each line to figure out whether we're skipping up or down!

Melodic or Harmonic?

Below are some chords. Some are written melodically, while others are written harmonically. Look at the chords in each measure below, and determine if it is arranged melodically or arranged harmonically. Circle the corresponding terms, Melodic or Harmonic.

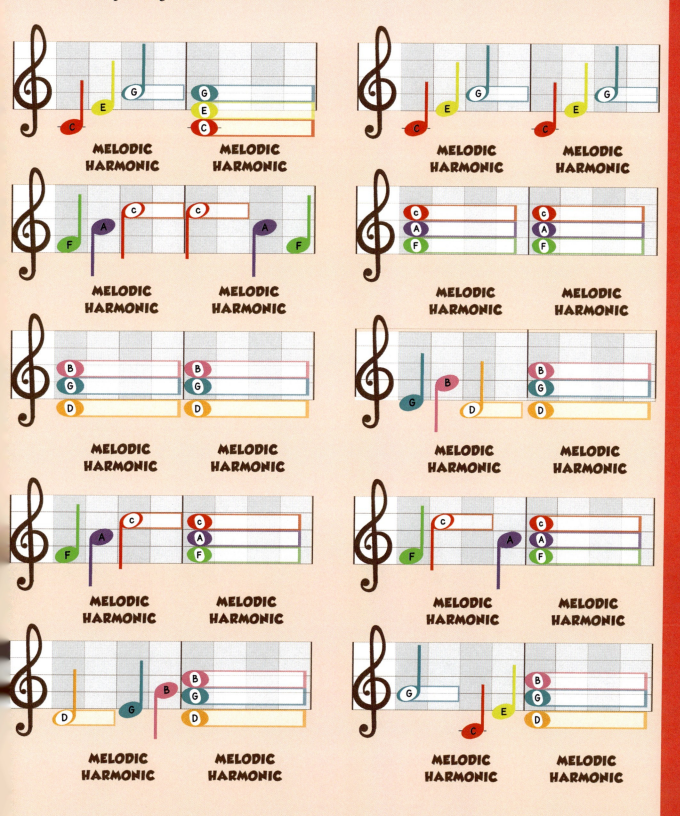

Write Your Own Duet!

Use the page below to write your own duet. In a duet, the Player 1 staff and Player 2 staff happen at the same time. That's why they're connected with a dark line on the left. Count "1, 2, ready, play" and then start the duet on beat 1 together. As you're writing your parts, play your instrument to make sure you like the way it sounds. Don't forget to use some rests in each line, that way each player has a couple notes to play all on their own.

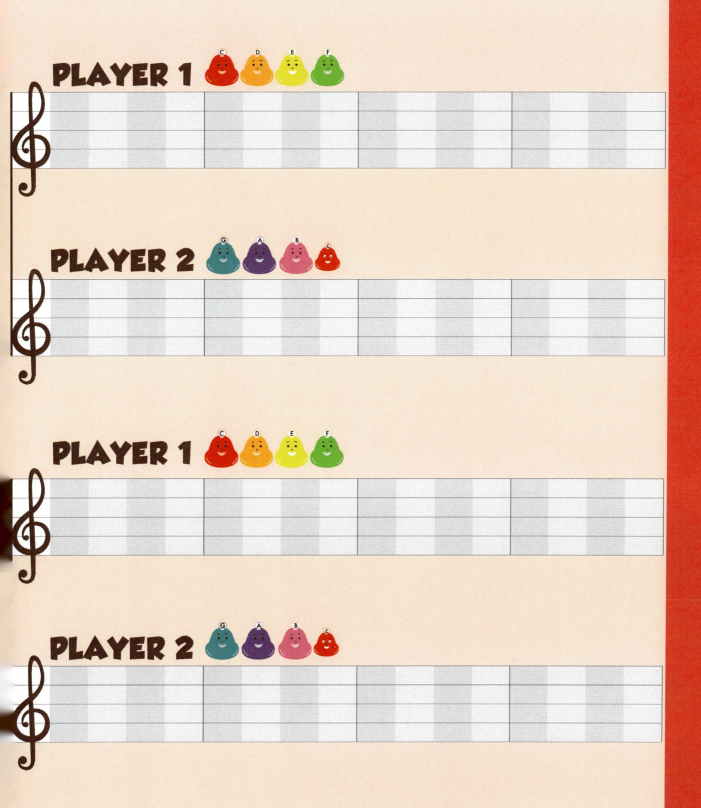

1.6 - Za Time

After you watch the 1.6 video, try playing along with the rhythm pizzas! Try clapping along with each rhythm and singing along with the different pizza terms and numbers.

CHORUS 1

We've got a crun-chy mun-chy piz-za pie,
We'll cut it up to make a slice!
Our oo-ey goo-ey piz-za pie,
Let's see how it di-vides.

VERSE 1

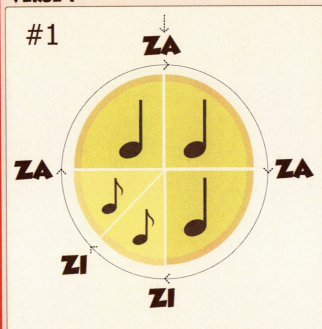
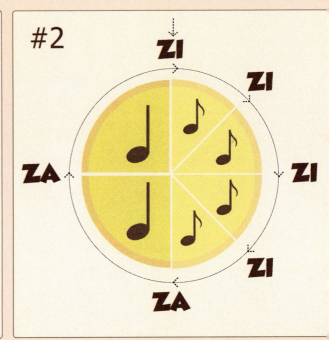
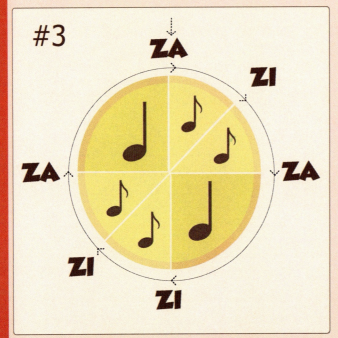
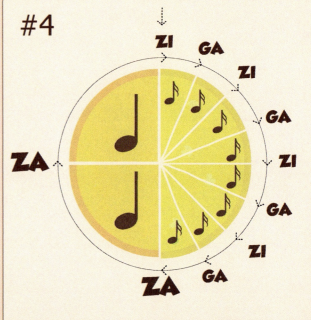

CHORUS 2

We've got a crun-chy mun-chy piz-za pie,
Which top-ping will you de-cide!
For our oo-ey goo-ey piz-za pie,
Cause now it's top-ping time.

VERSE 2

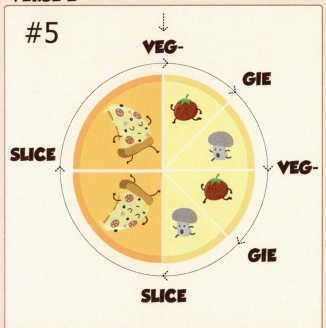

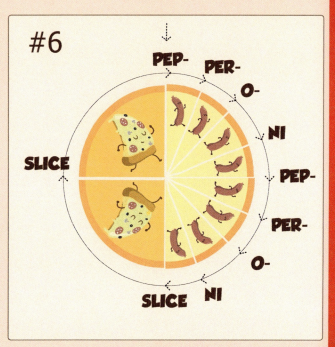

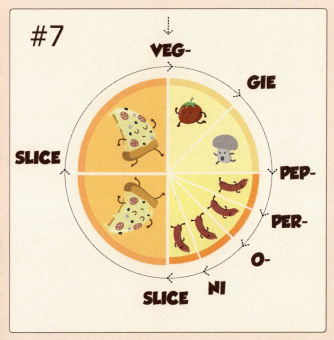

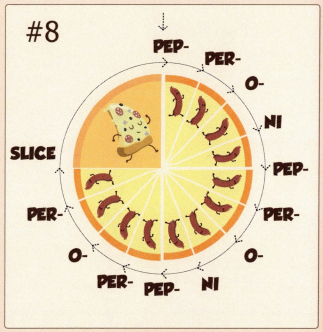

CHORUS 3

We've got a crun-chy mun-chy piz-za pie,
See how it loves to di-vide!
O-ur oo-ey goo-ey piz-za pie,
And now it's num-bers time.

VERSE 3

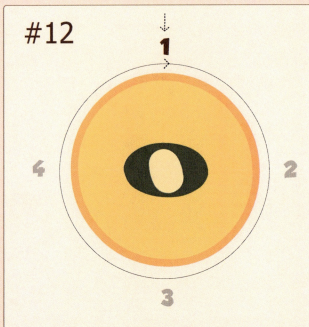

CHORUS 4

We've got a crun-chy mun-chy piz-za pie,
We'll cut it up to make a slice!
Our oo-ey goo-ey piz-za pie,
Let's see how it di-vides.

VERSE 4

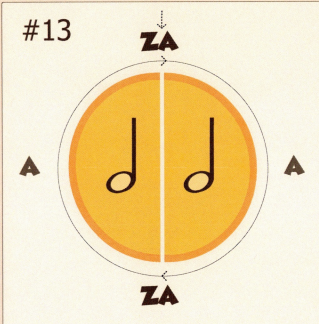

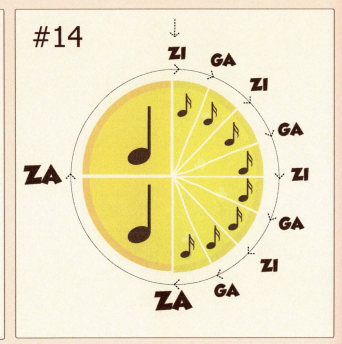

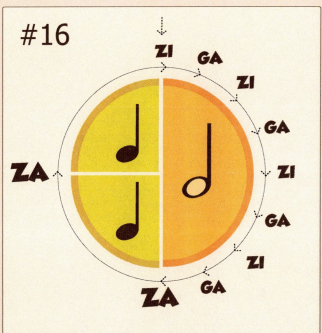

Easy As Pie ✏️

Let's make some fractions using our Pizza slices.
In the orange box, write <u>how many slices are in the pizza</u>. This will be the bottom number in our fraction.
Then, in the yellow box, write <u>how many slices have toppings.</u>
Then re-write your answers in the matching color boxes below.
And that's how you make fractions... easy as pie!

How many slices are in this pizza?
4

How many slices have toppings?
3

What fraction of the pizza has toppings?
3
4

How many slices are in this pizza?

How many slices have toppings?

What fraction of the pizza has toppings?

How many slices are in this pizza?

How many slices have toppings?

What fraction of the pizza has toppings?

How many slices are in this pizza?

How many slices have toppings?

What fraction of the pizza has toppings?

How many slices are in this pizza?

How many slices have toppings?

What fraction of the pizza has toppings?

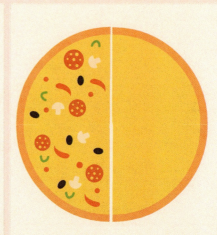

How many slices are in this pizza?

How many slices have toppings?

What fraction of the pizza has toppings?

Fraction Action

Fill in the blanks under each shape to write the number of shaded sections over the total number of parts of each shape. Be sure to include your answer in fraction form below each number.

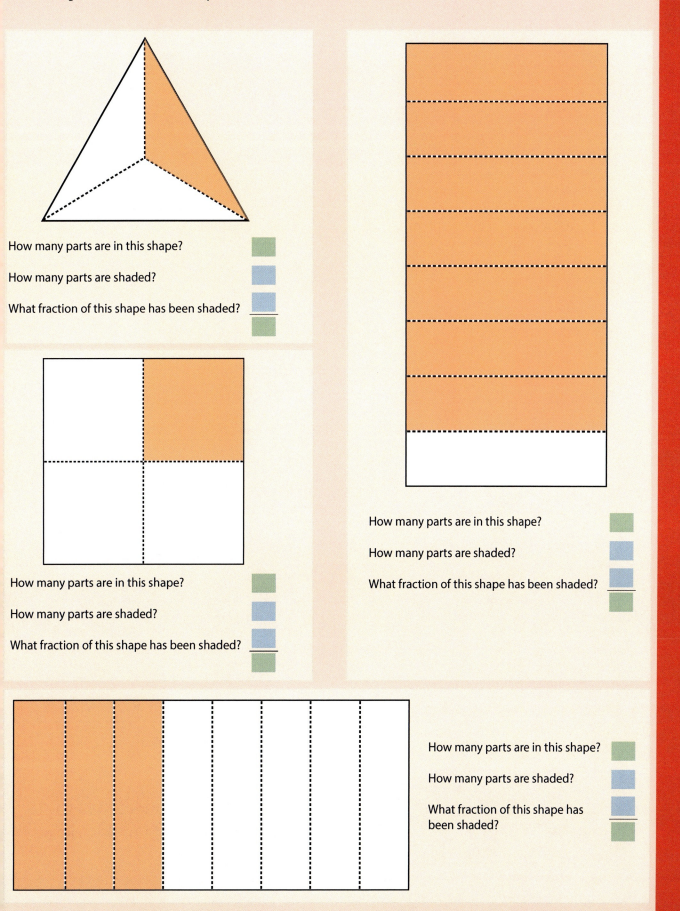

Color the Fraction

Color each shape to match each fraction below.

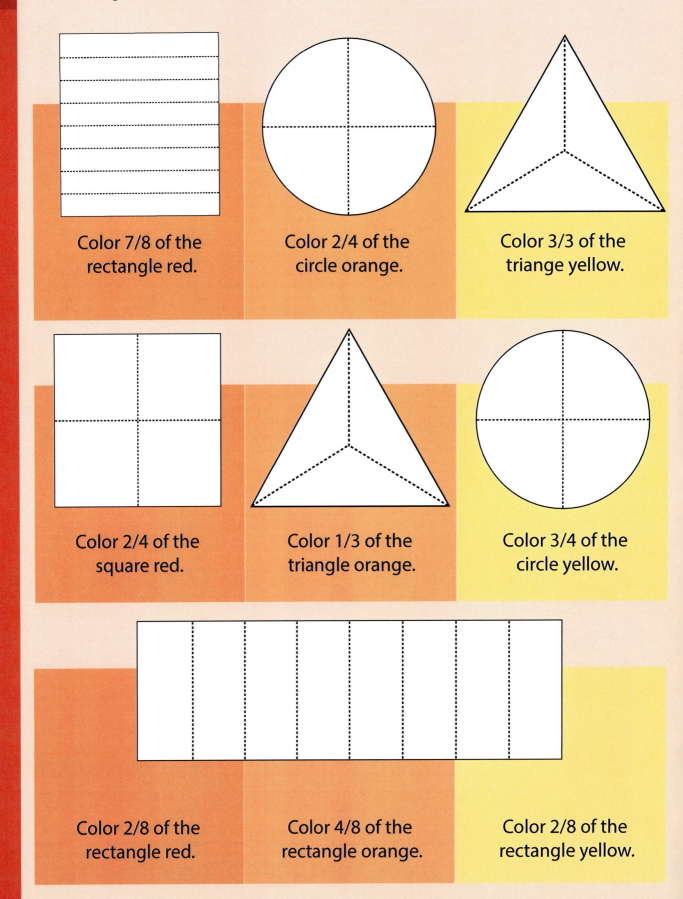

C Major Fractions

Answer each question below based on the C Major scale.

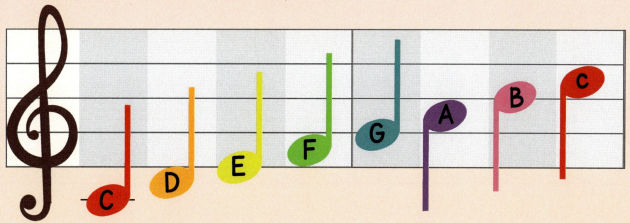

What fraction of notes are the color red?	What fraction of notes are the color orange?

What fraction of notes live on the staff?	What fraction of notes are in the G chord?

What fraction of notes live in the first measure?	What fraction of notes contain a C?

What fraction of notes live below the A?	What fraction of notes live above the A?

Rhythm Matching

In the following two matching activities, draw a line between each note and the fraction or pizza that represents it.

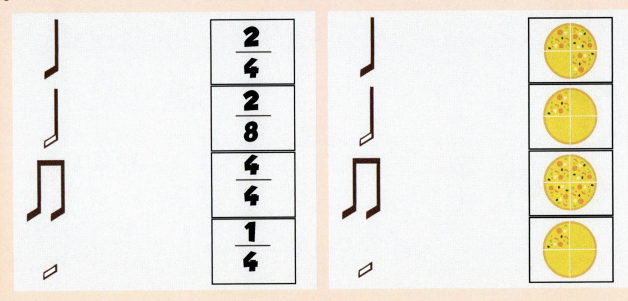

Do Something Rhythmic!

Use the following blank measures to write your own rhythm song. Clap, stomp, or snap out your rhythm after you've recorded it below. Then, try singing the ZA rhythm vocabulary along with your song!

Complete the Measure ✏️

Read each box below to determine the notes that are missing from each measure. Then, draw the missing notes in the correct place. If you're not sure, look at your answers from the matching game on the previous page.

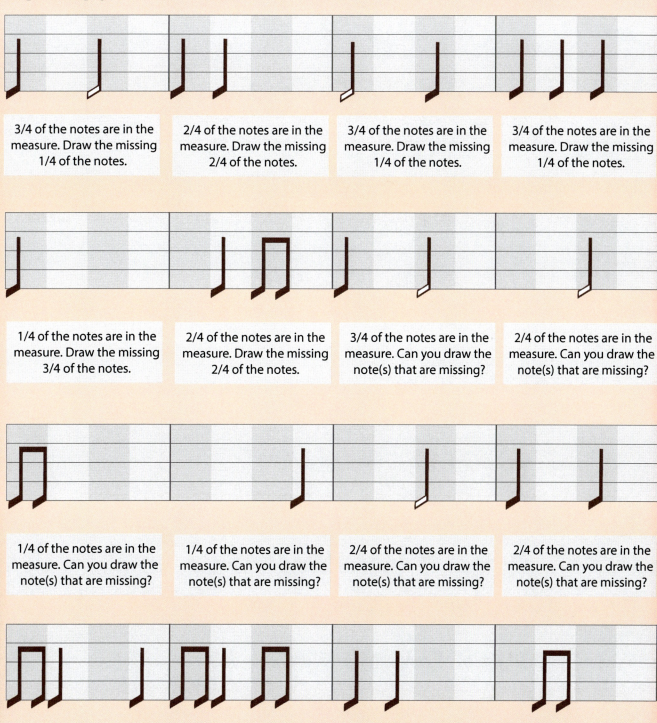

1.7 – Chord Review I, IV, V

After you watch the 1.7 video, try playing along with the following chord charts.

Sally the Camel

SALLY THE CAMEL HAS, FIVE HUMPS

SALLY THE CAMEL HAS, FIVE HUMPS

SALLY THE CAMEL HAS, FIVE HUMPS

SO RIDE, SALLY RIDE

London Bridge Is Falling Down

LONDON BRIDGE IS FALLING DOWN

FALLING DOWN, FALLING DOWN

LONDON BRIDGE IS FALLING DOWN

MY FAIR LADY

Lightly Row

C I **G** V
LIGHTLY ROW, LIGHTLY ROW

C I **G** V
OVER ALL THE WAVES WE GO

C I **G** V
SMOOTHLY GLIDE, SMOOTHLY GLIDE

C I **C** I
ON THE SILENT TIDE

G V **G** V
LET THE WIND AND WATERS BE

C I **C** I
MINGLED WITH OUR CHILDISH GLEE

C I **G** V
LIGHTLY ROW, LIGHTLY ROW

C I **C** I
IN OUR LITTLE BOAT.

Twinkle Twinkle Little Star

C^I **F**^{IV} **C**^I
TWINKLE TWINKLE LITTLE STAR

F^{IV} **C**^I **G**^V **C**^I
HOW I WONDER WHAT YOU ARE

C^I **F**^{IV} **C**^I **G**^V
UP ABOVE THE WORLD SO HIGH

C^I **F**^{IV} **C**^I **G**^V
LIKE A DIAMOND IN THE SKY

C^I **F**^{IV} **C**^I
TWINKLE TWINKLE LITTLE STAR

F^{IV} **C**^I **G**^V **C**^I
HOW I WONDER WHAT YOU ARE.

Roman Numeral Review

In music, we often refer to chords by using Roman numerals. The three chords we use are C, F and G, or in Roman numerals, I, IV and V. Roman numerals look like a combination of the letters I and V. The I stands for 1 and the V stands for five. To make a 4, we put a I before a V to show one before five. Complete the review below to make sure you feel comfortable with Roman numerals I, IV and V.

Roman Numeral Matching

Match the following Roman numerals to the numbers and bell groups that they represent.

Roman Numeral Groups

Circle the Roman Numeral that matches the number of treble clefs in each box.

Roman Numeral Problems

Complete each math problem below and write your answer in Roman numeral form.

4	3	0	3	2
+ 1	+ 2	+ 1	+ 1	+ 2
V				

| 6 | 2 | 7 | 8 | 9 |
| − 1 | − 1 | − 2 | − 4 | − 5 |

Chord Identification ✏️

Each of the following boxes represents either the I chord, the IV chord or the V chord. In the small box, write the Roman numeral represented in each group.

Complete the Chord ✏️

In each measure below, there is at least one note missing from the chord. Can you determine which note is missing? Write the note name in each whole note. In the second half of the activity, challenge yourself by naming two missing notes without the help of the bell colors.

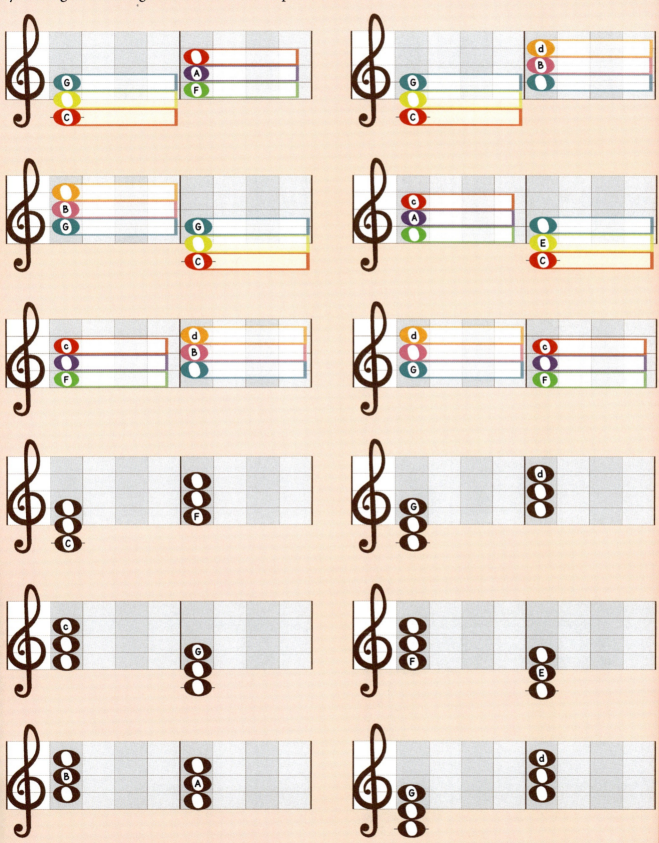

Piano Chords

Color or shade the piano keys on each keyboard that represent the chord indicated to the right.

Chord Building 📝

Using each root note pictured below, build the I, IV and V chords by adding the notes they are missing to each measure.

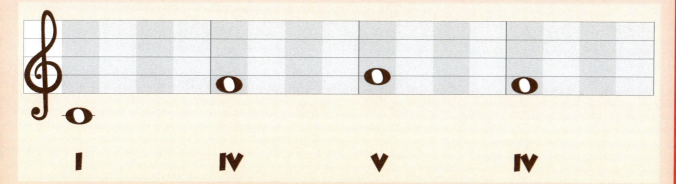

Write Your Own Chord Progressions 📝

Add one chord to each measure of the sheet music below to create your own chord progression. You can use each line to make a small chord progression, or you can use them all together to make a longer progression. You can stack chords harmonically, or arrange them melodically. It will sound a little bit more like a chord progression with harmonic chords.

1.8 – Lightly Row (Steps and Skips)

After you watch the 1.8 video, try playing along with the sheet music! You can use the sheet music to practice singing and playing the melody, or you can play the chords using the triangles below each measure. You can also hand-sign through the melody for extra singing practice!

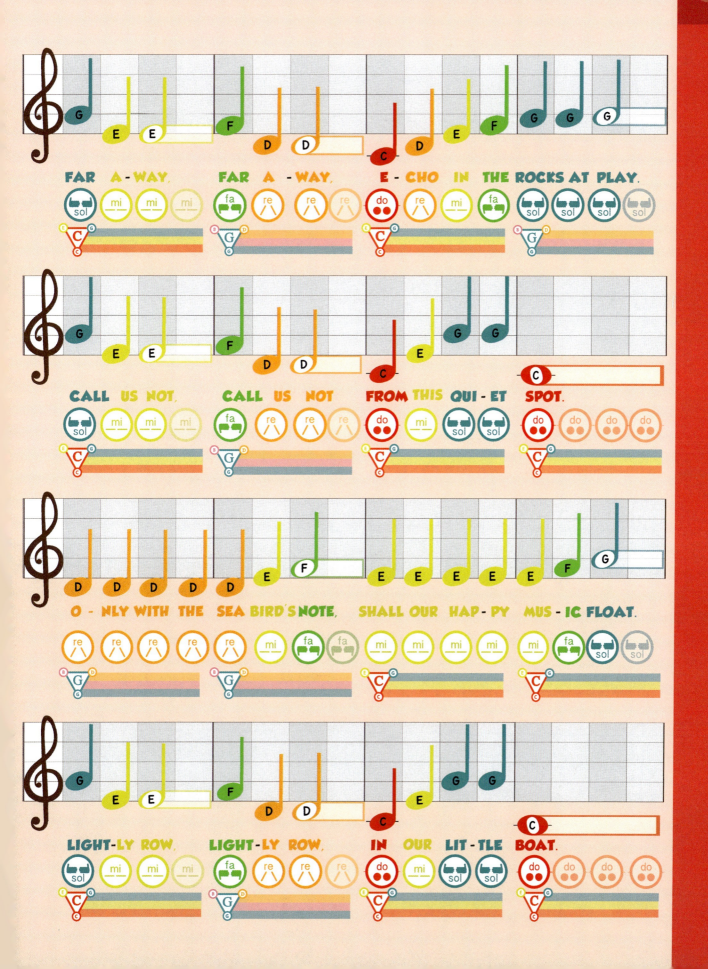

60 Steps or Skips? ✏️

Review the sheet music below from Lightly Row, then chose A, B or C to correctly identify the relationship between each pair of designated notes.

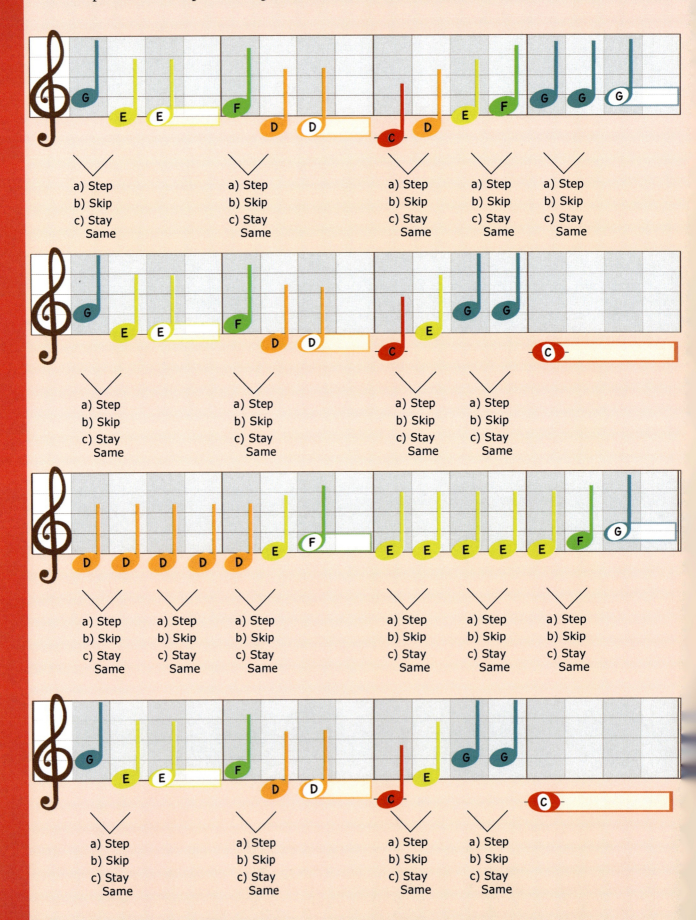

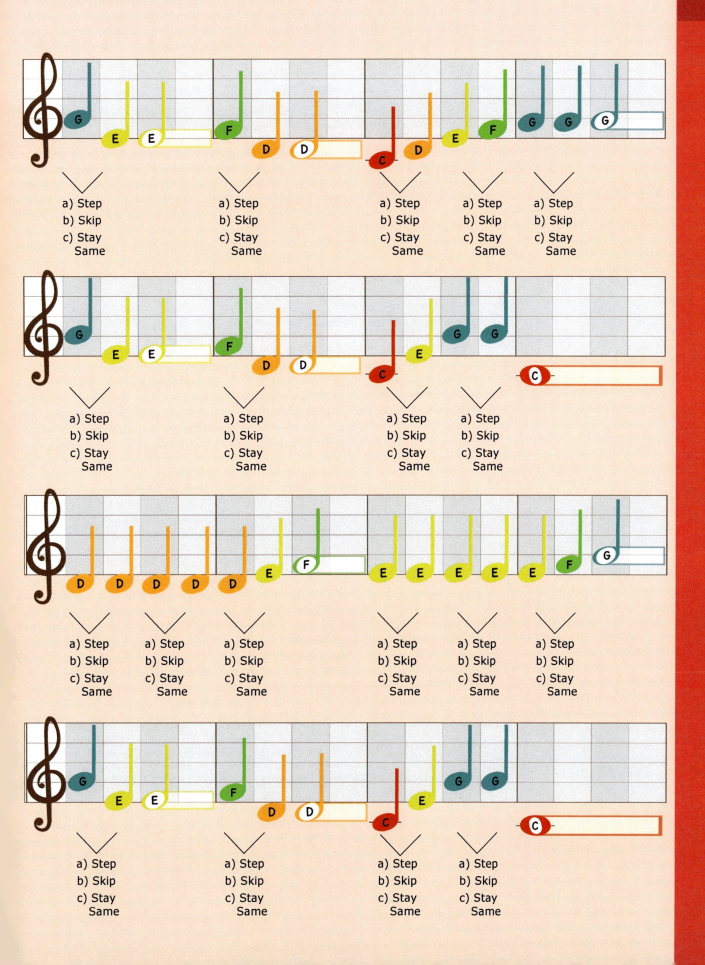

Skip or Step Up and Down

Using the scale degrees or numbers below, write the number that should come next based on the arrow. If it's a straight diagonal arrow, step up or down, and if it's a curved arrow, skip up or down.

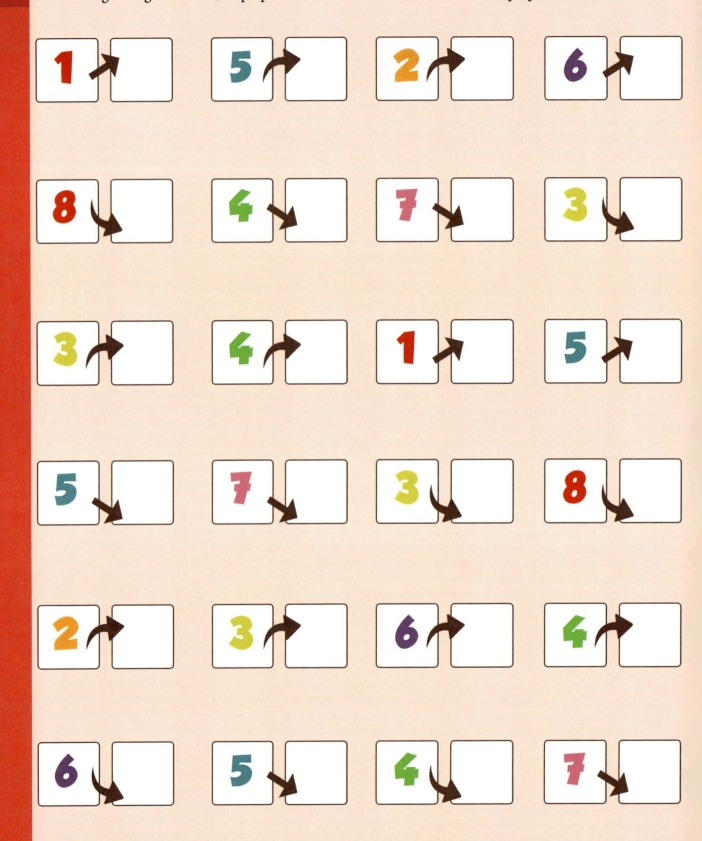

Circle the Steps and Skips

On the pianos below, you will circle either pairs of steps or pairs or steps. They can be any pair you want on the piano, as long as the circle is only connecting either the skips or steps!

Circle 3 musical skips on the piano below. ✏️

Circle 4 steps on the piano below. ✏️

Circle 4 skips below. ✏️

Write a Melody Based on Chords ✏️

Using the page below, write your own melody and try to use notes that match the chord triangle under each measure. You can mix it up and experiment a bit, but the chord-tones are a good place to start. If you want to use some F or B notes, try them over the G chord. You can also try A on top of both chords!

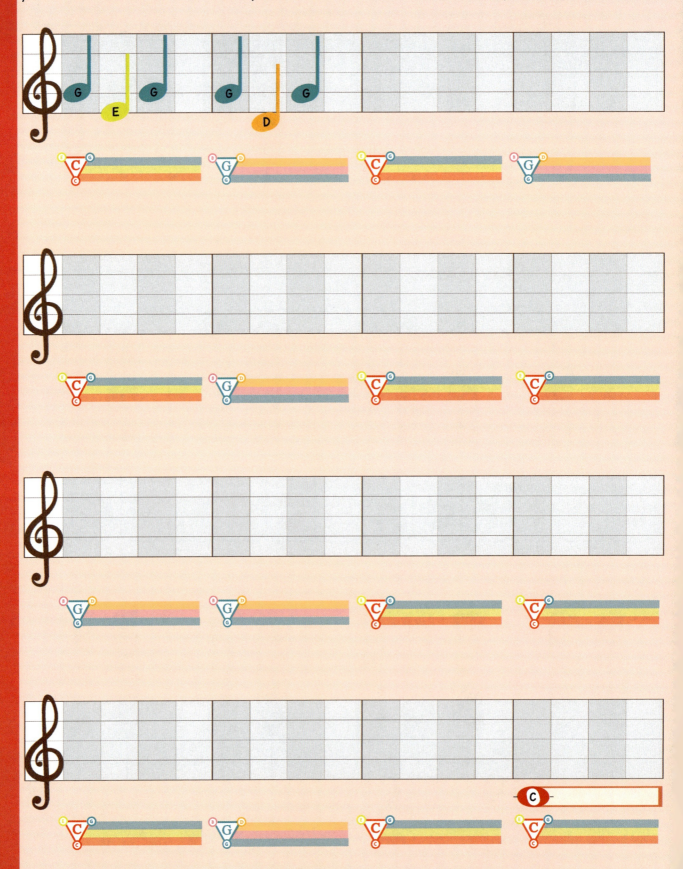

Skip or Step on the Keys ✏️

Look at the shaded keys and the small arrows below them. Are the notes a step apart or a skip apart? Write down the answer on the lines below the pianos.

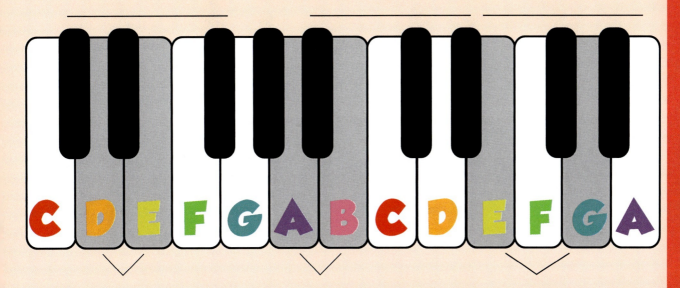

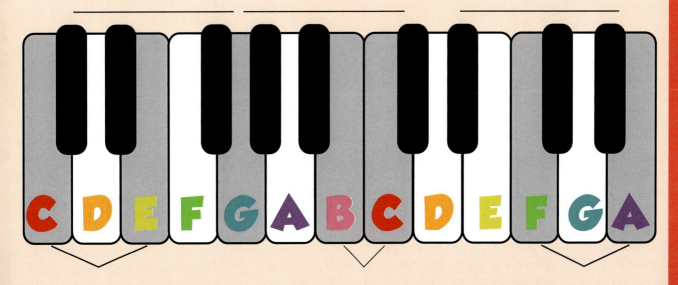

1.9 Rhythmic Dictation

A Rhythmic Dictation is a listening game for rhythm. In the video, Mr. Rob will play you a rhythm on a drum, and your job is to write it down. As he plays each rhythm, listen carefully first so you can learn the sound of the rhythm. Then, once you can sing the rhythm to yourself, try to write it down using the notes in the note bank.

Remember that there are four beats in each measure. Play attention to how many beats each note is worth and be sure to only use 4 total beats in each measure.

ROUND ONE

NOTE BANK:

1 Beat   2 Beats   4 Beats

1.

2.

3.

4.

5.

ROUND TWO

NOTE BANK:

1 Beat   1 Beat   2 Beats

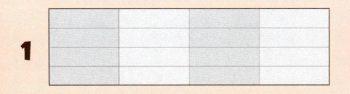

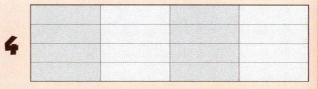

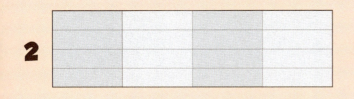

ROUND THREE

NOTE BANK:

1 Beat   1 Beat   1 Beat

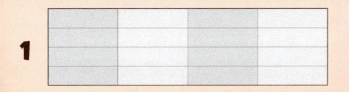

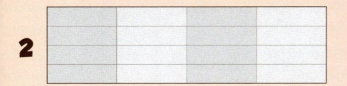

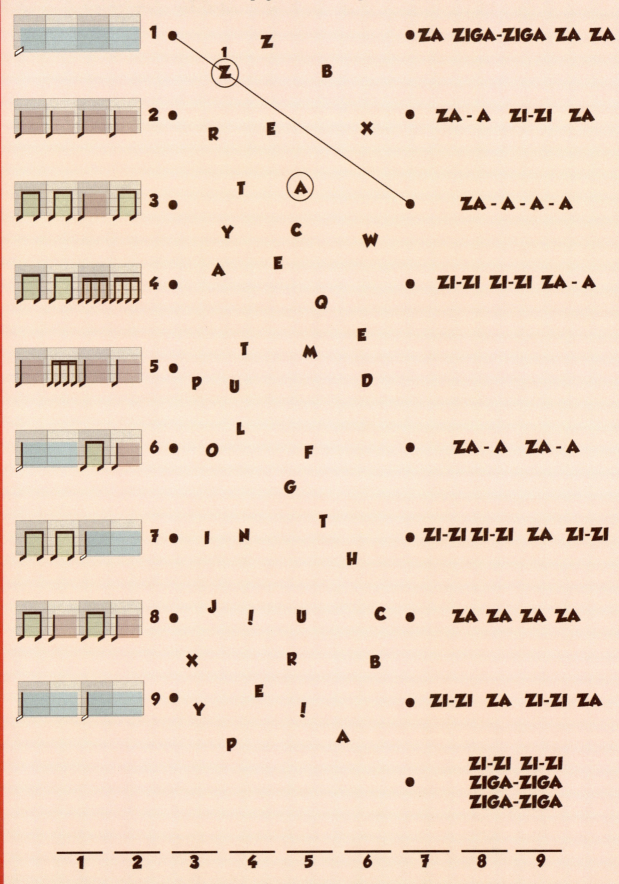

Beat Math ✏️

Add each group of beats below according to each musical note's value. Look back in the pizza section of this chapter if you're not sure how much each beat is worth.

𝅗𝅥 + ♪♪♪♪ + ♩ =

♩ + 𝅗𝅥 + ♫ =

♫ + ♩ + ♪♪♪♪ =

𝅗𝅥 + ♩ + 𝅗𝅥 =

♩ + ♩ + ♩ =

♩ + ♩ + ♪♪♪♪ =

♩ + ♩ + ♩ =

♫ + 𝅗𝅥 + ♩ =

♩ + ♩ + ♪♪♪♪ =

♫ + 𝅗𝅥 + ♩ =

♩ + ♩ + ♪♪♪♪ =

♩ + ♩ + ♩ =

♫ + ♩ + 𝅗𝅥 =

♩ + ♪♪♪♪ + ♩ =

♩ + ♩ + ♫ =

𝅗𝅥 + ♩ + 𝅗𝅥 =

Rhythm Cut-Outs ✂

Cut out each box on the next page, then complete the three activities below.

Activity One – Build a Rhythm

Using the rhythm cut-outs, arrange your own rhythms in any order you'd like. Then practice clapping, singing or stomping out your rhythms. Challenge yourself to move your rhythms from a simple pace to a more challenging pace.

Activity Two – Rhythmic Duets

With a partner, each person arranges a rhythm using their rhythm cut-outs. Then, each partner switches places and claps, sings or stomps the rhythm the partner has created. Take turns going back and forth playing each other's rhythms or try stringing longer rhythms together.

Activity Three – Call and Response Circle

This next activity is completed with a group of at least three people, and in rounds. Each student sits with his or her Rhythm Cut-outs. For each round, each student will create his or her own 4/4 rhythm. Once all students have created a rhythm, they take turns going around clapping their rhythm. After the first student claps his or her rhythm, the others will respond by clapping the same rhythm. Then the next student claps his or her reponse, and the class repeats that one, too. This goes on until each student has clapped his or her rhythm and the group has repeated it back. Then, each student creates new rhythms for round two and the group repeats the process. Eventually, each student will go around and clap his or her rhythm without the class clapping it back, so that it is one long, continuous rhythm.

Activity Four – Rhythmic Dictations

You can also use the cutouts to figure out the rhythmic dictations in the 1.9 video. Rhythmic dictations can be tricky, and you can always try some simple call and response with the rhythm and then work on piecing it together with the cutouts from there.

72

1.F Chapter One Review and Assessment

Review each section from Chapter One to see what you've learned! Are there any sections that you should review?

1.1 Review: Answer each question about the staff.

| How many lines are on a staff? | How many spaces are on a staff? |

Circle the note that is higher: A E

Circle the note that is lower: B D

1.2 Review: Trace each trebel clef, note, solfege name and scale degree.

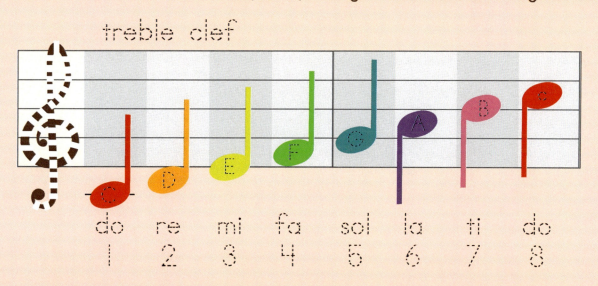

1.2 Review: Match each scale degree to the hand-sign it represents.

    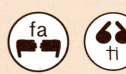

1.3 Review: Match the beats to their note, then practice adding the beats.

1.4-1.5 Review: Write the scale degree that comes next based on the arrow.

1.4-1.5 Review: Circle whether each measure is Melodic or Harmonic.

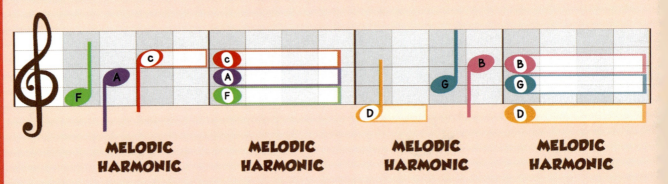

1.6 Review: Match each note to the fraction or pizza it represents on the staff. 📝

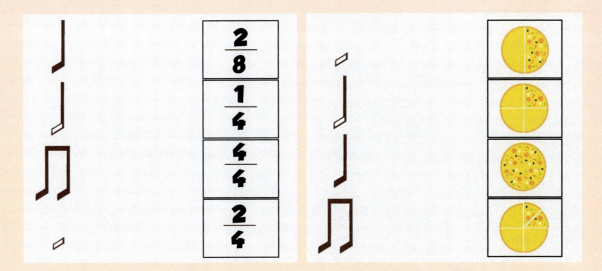

1.7 Review: Write the Roman Numeral that represents the chords in the measures below. 📝

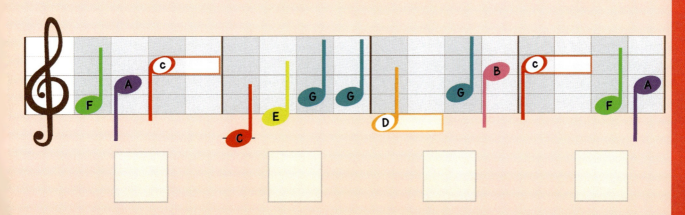

1.8 Review: Choose whether each set of identified notes is a skip, step or the same.

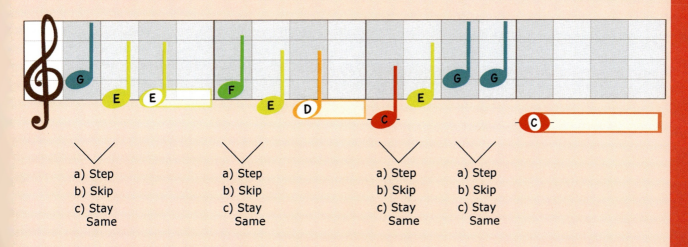

a) Step
b) Skip
c) Stay Same

a) Step
b) Skip
c) Stay Same

a) Step
b) Skip
c) Stay Same

a) Step
b) Skip
c) Stay Same

76

CONGRATULATIONS

....

Great work with

PRIMARY PRODIGIES

CHAPTER 1

....
Teacher Signature   Date

Made in the USA
Columbia, SC
02 October 2021